Dec. 1979

Best Wishes

Ginny

Bill Bennett.

PACIFIC DOGWOOD   Bruce A. Macdonald

COVER PHOTO

KENNEDY RIVER, VANCOUVER ISLAND   Clifford A. Fenner

BRITISH COLUMBIA
our Land

Words By Paul St. Pierre.

Photographs by some of the people who live in the land.

hancock
house

Copyright © 1977   Paul St. Pierre

ISBN 0-919654-96-7

Cataloging in Publication Data

St. Pierre, Paul, 1923-
    British Columbia

    ISBN 0-919654-96-7

    1. British Columbia — Description and
travel — Views. I. Title.
FC3812.S26   917.11'0022'2   C77-002153-0
F1087.8

Published simultaneously in Canada and the United States by Hancock
House Publishers, Saanichton, Toronto, Seattle.

Printed in Canada
Designed by NICHOLAS NEWBECK DESIGN

Published by:

Hancock House Publishers Ltd.

3215 Island View Road
SAANICHTON, B.C. V0S 1M0

Hancock House Publishers Inc.

12008 1st Avenue South
SEATTLE, WA. 98168

Almost 1000 people submitted over 10,000 photographs
to make this book possible. Space limitations
and the rules of our competition determined
the choice of photographs for this volume.

We were astonished and delighted by the high quality of
the photos and selected those which, in our mind, best conveyed
the variety and beauty of our land. To round out this
first volume of British Columbia photographs, additional
material was chosen from the publisher's resources and
from government agencies.

Thank you, all of you, who contributed to this book.
You made our job a pleasure.

The Publisher

Nature has indeed been generous to our homeland as the photographs in BRITISH COLUMBIA : OUR LAND graphically show.

However, each of us is in some measure responsible for the custodianship of this tremendous heritage that includes some of North America's grandest scenery and much of the world's significant mineral, lumber and fisheries production. Most importantly, also, it contains a rich blend of aboriginal and immigrant peoples.

Residency in British Columbia must be considered a blessing for its environmental advantages, social attitudes and its commercial opportunities.

Our land is a good land, but with opportunity comes responsibility— and how we British Columbians exercise this responsibility today will determine the real worth of our land tomorrow.

The contents of this book have been carefully and painstakingly chosen from the very best work of many people. The final selections have been assembled in an attempt to portray the immense diversity of our land known as British Columbia.

And Paul St. Pierre, one of our province's best-known writers, has compiled a moving narrative to accompany the magnificent photographs.

W. R. Bennett
Premier
Province of British Columbia

KENNEDY RIVER, VANCOUVER ISLAND

Clifford A. Fenner

The Ulgatchos rise blue above the green trees and yellow grass of the Anahim Highlands and in mellow autumn they are sleepy old mountains. Nearby is the chaotic heap of Matterhorn type peaks, hard granite and glacier, of the Coast Mountain system, the ones which local people call the hills with the crust on top. Time has dealt more gently with the Ulgatchos and has made smoother curves of their softer rock. Not much more than ten miles from side to side, they are remnants of a volcano, given over now to growing flowers in the brief summer and holding the lonely snows of winter for much of the rest of the year when men or animals no longer visit there. Two nights we had slept on the frosty grass of alpine meadows. Our campfires were a few handfuls of dead alpine pine, little stunted and twisted trees which had fought the winds and snows here for a century or more to grow to the height of a boy.

Their wood was heavy in pitch and raged while it burned, but the fire was brief, like our own incursion into these hills. The slopes are never gentle when you climb them and every ridge we climbed burned the body's stores of energy as rapidly as flames consumed the campfire wood at night.

On the third morning, we sat for a time on the thin grass of a sidehill and looked over a few hundred square miles of country with a strange complacency which seems common to all British Columbia people; we seem to develop a capacity for acting as if we made our mountains and arranged our weather.

There were three of us: Pan Philips, who in the 1930s with his partner Rich Hobson carved out the Home Ranch which lay a couple of thousand feet below our boots; Bill Lampert, who was attempting to start another ranch nearby on the banks of the Blackwater River; and myself, a wandering wordsmith.

Pan began naming the lakes, the rivers and creeks and the swathes of swamp meadow beneath us. There was the Blackwater River, which was also known as the West Road River, a name commemorating the trip by Sir Alexander Mackenzie in 1793. He was the first white man to cross the North American continent north of Mexico. Not far from this river beside which Mackenzie had walked, often hungry because he found the game scarce, was Stuyvesant Lake. The original Peter Stuyvesant was a fur trader whose name was made famous in the Columbia River country far to the south. It was a descendant of his who left his name here in the 1930s after helping finance Philips and Hobson in their Frontier Cattle Company venture.

The creek beside the ranch was named Pan Creek. The one we had ascended was Cadwallader, named for a creek Pan had lived beside during his boyhood in Ohio. Rich Creek was for Rich Hobson, dead two years before our visit with one of those sudden heart attacks which wink out the lives of lucky men. Alexi Lake was for Peter Alexi, an Indian who ran cows there, and Lester Meadow for Lester Dorsey of Anahim Lake, who once harnessed thirteen unbroken cayuses in line and tried to plow it. Shag Creek was for Shag Thomson, a cowboy who tried to ranch there until more sensible ideas sent him into the real estate trade. Happy Jack Creek was for his brother, another man who tried.

The mountainside on which we sat had been there for a couple of million years. The caribou had ranged it since the last retreat of the glaciers about 10,000 years ago. The Indians had hunted here occasionally since and perhaps before—nobody knows how many thousands of years ago the first settlers crossed the Bering land bridge and began populating the western continents. Yet of the names on today's map, the names Pan was quoting as we sat on that sidehill, almost every one was linked to people whom I knew personally, and I had come to British Columbia in 1945.

Of the three of us there that morning, my companions were the adventurers. They had come into raw country and tried to live on it and with it. They had been familiar with cold and privation and sometimes had unexpected conversations with grizzly bears.

I was the more typical British Columbian of today. My home was in Greater Vancouver where almost half of all the people of the province live. For most of my years mountains offered a colorful background for the lights of the big city and they sheltered me from the cold winds of the north; most of my daily wants were satisfied by pushing buttons or using a telephone and a garbage collector's strike was about the largest natural disaster likely to strike. In most of this province it is only when above the timberline that the eye ever gets a chance to see a horizon that curves or to gain any true sense of spaciousness, yet this was the first time in several years that I had gone so high and it was to be a full five years before I did so again.

All of us, all men, have touched this land only briefly and recently. Nobody owns it. We use little bits of it, here and there, and after a lifetime we depart leaving it sometimes better and often worse.

It is far too big for us to know it. Neither have we yet settled it. The Indians, who have prior claim, were few. They trickled through the passes, lived on the fish in the lower valleys and collected in a few tiny bands on beaches between the dark forest and the deep sea. Men who followed them in greater numbers have settled in the same patterns—a few rivulets and pools of humanity in the valley bottoms and on the seashore. We live among the mountains, but not on them. We venture into them, as we three did that weekend, to snatch from them something we want and retreat to the safety and comfort of our lowlands. Among the mountains, which are the heart and soul of this land, men are still as scant as a handful of carelessly loosed arrows.

Our sense of proprietorship is absurd. Our vision is too confined to the many countries of the mountains. Our sense of time is too warped to comprehend the ages which made the land what it is today and which are remaking it for tomorrow.

If there are to be people who can be said to know and understand this land, they have not yet been born nor may we expect to see them for centuries or more. Meanwhile we live here unsurprised that the wild land tolerates us and often we are without the saving grace of humility.

Our thought processes may be wrong. Western man, we are told, has a prediliction for linear reasoning and a distrust of the intuitive. The Indian could arrive at conclusions by visionary thought which he expressed poetically without offering his calculations for examination and debate. Thus Chief Seattle of the Duwamish Indians of Washington State could write to an American president in 1855, "All things share the same breath—the beasts, the trees, the man. The white man does not seem to notice the air he breathes. Like a man dying for many days, he is numb to the stench…The whites, too, shall pass—perhaps sooner than other tribes…We might understand if we knew what it was that the white man dreams, what hopes he describes to his children on the long winter nights, what visions he burns into their minds, so they will wish for tomorrow. But we are savages. The white man's dreams are hidden from us."

Is it pretty turning of phrases or is it a terrible, true vision, born of mourning? We do not know but it speaks well of things beyond ordinary understanding and surely this land of British Columbia is beyond ordinary understanding. We see the land but briefly and fitfully. Most of the time we huddle at the mountain's feet and make ourselves busier and busier about less and less.

To gain some understanding takes many years. Some of us live out our lives here and never find the time. Oddly enough, the perceptive air traveller may learn more in an hour than do those on the ground in a decade. Whether it be night or day matters little to the air traveller. If it be night, he may identify the lights of some city floating below the whispering jet; by day he may see that city wrapped in the bows and ribbons of freeways or he may see only a brown smog which is the mark of its prosperity. He may see squared fields of farmlands, lakes drawn in nature's imprecise patterns or the endless march of the evergreen forest which is Canada's taiga. The scene is distant, inhuman and in some way irrelevant.

The traveller of experience takes a seat on the aisle, where one elbow at least will be free, he tucks his shoes in the pocket with the vomit bags, reads something torpid in hope of inducing fitful slumber or watches movies on the bulkhead. Few forms of travel quite so disinteresting have been developed since Britain sent the convict ships to Australia.

Flying over the mountains is one exception if it be done on one of the rare days when clouds don't hide most or all of them. Seven miles, the usual cruising altitude of a jet, gives a good perspective of the mountains. The observer can see variety as well as pattern. The marks of human settlement as well as its scars are set forth to the air traveller in true perspective. Even the many climate zones which are created by the folded landscape can be recognized. With a smattering of scientific knowledge the observer may gain some appreciation of the forces which tumbled this land into a choppy sea of stone.

A flight from Calgary to Vancouver will serve to illustrate a section of the Canadian Cordillera across its southern extremity, but the general pattern does not vary much from there to the borders of the Yukon.

At the edge of Calgary the prairie folds in a few pine clad foothills. Out of this the Rockies make their startling leap for the sky. They are the most famous Canadian mountains, so much so that the name is sometimes applied to all the mountains to the west of them, but to most of the rest the Rockies bear little resemblance. These mountains are sheets and wedges of striated rock from the bed of an inland sea. They have been sheared, twisted, folded and heaped on edge like split cedar. As with all the major ranges of the Canadian Cordillera, they run approximately north and south, bending to the west in their northern extremities. All these ranges therefore lie across or aslant west-to-east flow of the atmosphere at these latitudes. The climatic effect at ground level of this juxtaposition of rock against wind is immense. The Chinook wind, which is composed of air heated mechanically by compression in passage over certain mountain ranges, is but a small and capricious token of a vastly larger and more important process. The Rockies in this, their southern extremity, are less than seventy-five miles wide. At cruising speed a jet crosses them in less than ten minutes.

Dividing the Rockies from the next mountain range is the

plowmark of the Rocky Mountain Trench. From a rocket departing this planet it would, like China's Great Wall, be among the last clearly delineated features to be seen before everything diminished to general clutter. Five to ten miles wide, flat bottomed, it extends practically the length of the Rockies and it is as easy to recognize from the air as it is difficult from the ground. The surface traveller may cross and recross the Trench without being aware of its existence. He may stop his car where the highway turns on some promontory of the hills on either side and remark that here is a valley wide and beautiful but only from a great height can he apprehend the length and unusual regularity, an orderly strip amid the wild disorder of the mountain peaks.

The Purcells are the western bank of the Trench and next to them the Selkirks. Geologists consider these part of the same mountain system, together with others, including the massive Ominecas and Cassiars to the north. They are older than the Rockies, greener and jumbled rather than set fencelike. They are richer in the goods men prize. The Rockies have never yielded anything in quantity for the industrial world except coal. The Columbias have silver, lead, zinc and other materials on which a modern economy rolls.

The air traveller will see other subsidiary mountain ranges as he hurtles westward. All are intersected deeply, north and south, by large rivers and long thin lakes which mark the widening of those rivers. The little tributary streams come out of every fold of every mountain. They froth white in the spring's thaw, hide beneath the foliage of summer and in some of their reaches become dry in the year's hottest weeks and leave only the white boulders to mark their tumbling trail.

When the air traveller crosses the Okanagan he will see a wide valley, large blue lakes, rich green orchards where the irrigation ditch divides the desert from the sewn-in straight and precise lines. Beyond that the traveller sees pale yellow grass hills and scattered Ponderosa and Lodgepole pines. Again, although now less recognizably, he is crossing a well-defined region of western North America. The intermontane belt is a dry plateau of rolling hills and little rain or snow. It begins near Mexico, extends between the mountain ranges in California, Nevada, Oregon and Washington states and here, in its northern reaches carries its scrubby cactus and blue-gray sagebrush northward until the trees surround and extinguish it in the northern portion of the Cariboo-Chilcotin plateau.

Again, the plane crosses more mountains. First the Cascades, then the Coast, indistinguishable one from the other to the casual eye.

Nearing the Pacific, the forest beneath the aircraft becomes ever heavier and darker. The lower Fraser Valley, a green wedge of farmland, is driven eastward into the mountains from the river's delta on the Strait of Georgia. The Strait itself, marked by a fan of brown water at the river's mouth, is one more of the series of channels which have divided range from range. This one, unlike the others, is drowned in salt water and its scattered hilltops protrude as islands.

Beyond are the last of the mountain chains, forming Vancouver Island and the distant Queen Charlottes. Beyond those snow topped peaks is the open Pacific Ocean, unseen to the air traveller as it, by strange chance, remains unseen to almost all the people who live in British Columbia. The first public road to reach the western ocean met the surf for the first time in the 1950s at Long Beach on the western coast of Vancouver Island and it remains the only paved and well-travelled road to the ocean. Thousands of British Columbians get their first sight of the great North Pacific when they visit the beaches of Oregon State and hundreds of thousands of British Columbians live and die here having never seen nor heard the open sea.

The trip from east to west has taken one hour. Were the traveller flying from west to east the plane would probably consume fifty-five minutes for the same flight for it would fly with the prevailing westerly winds instead of against them. To these mountains, the prime reality of this land, must be added two others. They are the ocean, and the river of air which it spills over us. It is from that ocean that the warm, wet winds come, warming much of the western face of the land and piling snows to depths of sixty feet on the mountains' shoulders. In a land much devoted to myths, few are more common than the story that the warm Japanese Current washes our shores and takes the chill from the land's stony cold heart. Most of the waters which touch British Columbia, either on its western edge or in the intricate fretwork of fiords, are cold. The current called the Subarctic sweeps south from the Aleutians and, summer or winter, it is seldom warmer than eight degrees celsius. The fiords are fed by snow water from the glaciers.

We are warmed not by the water but by the winds. A weather pattern which, to judge by the evidence of tree growth, has persisted for many centuries, has a more or less constant low pressure area located south of the Aleutian Islands. The west winds bend southerly around this dimple of the weather map. They absorb heat and moisture from the warm Pacific waters north of Hawaii and then sweep in upon Northern California, Oregon, British Columbia and the Alaska Panhandle. There is a multitude of variations in this pattern and within the mountains there are microclimates, for each mountain is said to create its own weather. The general pattern remains and it is a simple one. As the warm, expanded and moisture-laden air crosses the mountain barriers it is lifted. As it lifts it cools and is unable to retain the moisture which forms cloud and rain. The western slopes of the mountains are blanketed by clouds and soaked for most of each year from sunless skies. The rain forest is brooding and dark, for the most part silent, to some ominous.

Only the higher peaks escape the snows and rains and the frantic growth of vegetation they promote. These pinnacles rise above the rain-bearing winds, hard gray stone tips bare in the thin, sterile upper air.

As the plane circles to land on Sea Island, one of the sandbanks of the Fraser's delta, the traveller may also glimpse an astonishing succession of climates which occur where winds and mountains meet.

To the west are the Gulf Islands, where grass is always green, our isles of Avalon where there is not sleet nor rain and seldom winds blow harshly. In an average year the islands will have a precipitation, almost all in the form of rain, of only about twenty-five to thirty-five inches. The annual mean temperature is nine degrees celsius. Meteorologists class the climate as North Mediterranean.

The delta on which the plane lands is closer to the mountains and feels their effect. Precipitation at the Vancouver airport will average forty-two inches although annual mean temperature is about the same as in the Gulf.

Beside the airport is Vancouver City, five miles wide. On its western slope there is an average of fifty-seven inches of precipitation and on the harbor front, closer to the mountains, it is sixty inches. Across the harbor in North Vancouver the waterfront records an average of seventy-nine inches. Three miles up the hillside 100 inches is common, and five miles farther, on Lynn Creek where the mountains begin, 114 inches falls in an average year.

About fifty miles distant from the airfield may be seen Garibaldi Mountain at the head of the Howe Sound fiord. There is a glacier there with alpine meadows at its feet which could be described as tundra, for there the climate is classified as Arctic. Within less than seventy-five miles are to be seen not one country but several, different in vegetation as in climate.

Birds and animals migrate across these zones. As elsewhere in Canada, we are familiar with north-south migrations of many species. In our land there is another, vertical migration. Many birds and animals migrate each spring from the lowlands to the highlands. The same instinct which sends the caribou of the Northwest Territories on treks of 500 miles also moves the Osborn Caribou of the Coast Ranges, but only five or ten miles.

From the Vancouver airport the eye can follow the endless river of the air only to the crest of the Coast Mountains, but this pattern is repeated across all the Cordillera. Immediately behind the crest of the Coast Mountains the air, milked of most of its moisture, leaves the ground arid beneath it. The rain shadow we call it. The change is abrupt. In ten miles of highway travel the rain jungle may be left behind and replaced by lands so dry that the condition verges upon desert.

Moving ever eastward, the dry winds suck moisture from rivers, lakes and trees, climb yet another mountain chain to release it, and again repeat the process at the other side—the western faces of the ridges thick in green growth, the eastern rain shadow sere and yellow.

Within this general climate pattern are innumerable variations. Individual mountains and clusters of mountains will inhale and exhale gusty local winds through their canyons. Small valleys may have microclimates. A steep mountain, south facing, may act as a radiator beneath the sun while a creek, frothing in its haste to get to the sea, constantly dampens the airs on the lower slopes. There, alone in a monocultural faunal and floral region, there may develop species exotic to that region in weather quite foreign to the prevailing pattern. There are sudden and violent cold winds which come out of some mountain passes like freight trains. The Alaskans call them williwaws; we call them Squamish winds. We may even complain of them, although in their brisk way they serve us well in sweeping away stagnant air which in the settled regions may be blue with the smoke of slash burning or brown with the sour breath of cities.

There are other, gentler winds. Katabatic winds, to give them their proper name, are the mountain people's equivalent of the sea breeze which cools those who live beside the oceans. No matter what the heat or humidity of a summer day, guardian mountains will have held cool air on their crests. At dark on some mountains, earlier on others, this air begins its drift down the slopes to the valley. Less than a wind or a breeze, it comes with the faintest whispering of leaves, and standing under the open sky a man is conscious of the change of temperature in the cool kiss of moving air on his cheek. It is like a sigh of a land preparing for restful sleep.

So, in a single hour, the air traveller has seen, however briefly, most of the many lands which make the mountain country. He has not seen the winds, but he has seen a land apparently frozen in wild convulsion. It may seem elemental as the sun, moon and stars, and as unchangeable, but that too, is an illusion.

No man can stand in the same river twice. Neither can he ever find mountains which are immobile and unchanging. In that single hour of flight, all of those mountains have altered and they will never again be exactly as they were when he first saw them, for all rock is plastic and all is, like the ocean waves, in constant motion. That we cannot perceive the motion makes it no less real but we are separated from that reality by our limited perception of the dimension of time. Our universe is two universes, existing together. With our limited sense of time we perceive a world in which waves move and trees sway, but the rocky frame of earth is fixed and solid. That is because if this solar system of ours, 4.6 billion years of age, had grown in a single year, human civilization would have begun while the clock was striking the last note of midnight on December 31. With a capacity to perceive time in the billions of years, we could visualize the land rising and falling beneath the seas, the Ice Ages coming and going like light morning frosts and the mountains themselves emerging and being swept down as if North America were a heavy carpet being pushed along a floor with its western edge wrinkling.

In the past decade man's knowledge of the movements of earth's crust appears to have taken one of the sudden leaps peculiar to the art of scientific investigation. What is called the plate theory has gained almost universal acceptance. (Neither this nor any other theory is ever accepted in the scientific community as an article of faith. Faith may be comforting but it is doubt which gives us an education and from the scientific doubts of today will come, some time, another leap of the imagination into a new and more satisfying theory.)

The plate theory envisages both the continents and the floors of the oceans being disconnected plates of cooler, more brittle rock, afloat upon a more plastic material. Forces dimly understood acted upon a single supercontinental plate about 200,000,000 years ago. Because it is our nature to disbelieve anything we can not name, science has given a name to this proto-continent. It is called Pangaea. Pangaea split first into two masses called Laurasia and Gondwana Land. There were more fracturings. The present continents of Eurasia, Africa, North and South America, Australia and Antarctica began a migration which has never ceased. The North American plate now migrates westward, crumpling where it thrusts against the oceanic plates of the Pacific.

There are three main processes at work where earth's plates meet, and all of them may be observed when spring ice floes move in a creek. Some plates collide to shatter and buckle.

Others draw apart, allowing the material beneath to well up. In the third process, plates slide one under another, tilting and fracturing. All these processes occur in the Canadian Cordillera which, with the Andes and the Himalayas, shares the status of being among the youngest mountain systems on the planet.

In the southwest corner of the province where more than three quarters of today's population lives, a small plate called the Juan de Fuca has been sliding beneath the mainland Coast Mountains for as little as ten or as much as one hundred and fifty million years. As the eastern edge of the Juan de Fuca plate slid eastward and downward it raised the Coast Mountains. It continues to slide beneath our feet today. The friction between its upper surface and the lower surface of the continental plate creates heat of which the visible evidence is a chain of volcanoes beginning at Mount Baker in Washington State and extending about 100 miles northeasterly to Mount Monmouth in the Bridge River district.

The volcanoes have not erupted in historic times. The last activity at Garibaldi was about 10,000 years ago. In the north near the Skeena River there was a volcanic explosion at just about the time the first Spanish explorers saw our shores in the mid-Eighteenth Century. We are reminded of the friction generated beneath our feet by hot springs, by occasional wisps of steam at Mount Baker and by the frequent jiggling of the seismograph needles.

A different plate movement involves the main North American and Pacific Ocean plates. The oceanic plate moves northwesterly at a rapid and quite irresistible six centimeters a year. Similar in nature to the infamous San Andreas fault of California, a fault line on the western side of the Queen Charlotte Islands rumbles with small tremors while movement is more or less continuing and threatens a dangerous earthquake should that shifting of the Pacific plate be temporarily halted long enough for severe tensions to be generated.

An earlier and similar stately procession of the plates of this planet's crust brought Vancouver Island against these shores from elsewhere. Baja and a portion of American California move in a similar slow waltz.

Within our continental plate there are also movements similar to these at the continent's edge, at least as laymen view such vast processes as the building of mountains. The Rockies, as might be expected, had one of the most colorful and dramatic births. The origin of this range begins with the great Precambrian Shield. We think of the Shield as a vast peneplane of ancient stone surrounding Hudson's Bay, the prairies forming a boundary on the west, the Great Lakes, Ottawa Valley and St.

Lawrence Rivers being boundaries of the south and east and the Arctic forming the northern limits.

The Precambrian Shield, we now know, has its western edge deep under the little town of Cranbrook in the Rocky Mountain Trench. Where the prairies and the Rocky Mountains now cover the Shield was an immense inland sea, on the bed of which sediment of the ages and aeons collected and solidified to rock. When the Columbia mountains began to thrust against these rocks they were forced up. Some of the sedimentary rock has bent and much has broken. The forces involved are as inconceivable to our sense as is the time and it may be suggested that to mortal men, song or poetry may serve as well to describe them as the language of the scientist.

As each of the main mountain groups have risen, the forces of wind, water, chemical and ice began to tear them down. Could we compress half a billion years to a ten minute movie, we would see the mountains grow to their present shapes, gullied ever deeper by streams, chiselled and sometimes smothered in waves of ice. This they do even now, however imperceptibly, before our unseeing eyes.

But all these are exercises of our imagination. The universe of our time frame, the land of here and now, is the one with which practical men must deal. In practical terms we know that the mountains and the seas are obstinate in resisting our effort to change them. Immense the land may be, but less than six million acres are good potential agricultural land and much of this is in pockets distant from centers of population and unmarked by the plow. We grow less than half the food needed by the 2,300,000 people who live here. This has always been so, not only for men but for the beasts.

The Cordillera contains a variety of wild animals unmatched by any other region of North America but for most of their tenure here their numbers have been small. Periodically a harsh winter and a late and icebound spring will send deer and moose down to the lowest elevations of the valleys among the houses of man and, if the growth of a new year comes too late, they starve to death. Only a little more than a century ago immense herds of elk disappeared from a large portion of the Cariboo plateau, leaving windrows of bones and antlers but no conclusive evidence of what natural calamity overtook them.

The Indians were not numerous. Neither were there any large regions of sufficient fertility for them to establish themselves in such numbers as to build civilizations on the scale attained by the associated people of Mexico, Central America, Peru or southwestern Ontario. Other men came by sea, the first perhaps Hoey Chin and his band of Buddhist monks about 500 A.D., later the Spanish and British explorers and the British and American men of commerce. Fur traders were drawn here overland from the east and south at about the same time Europeans approached the Pacific shores in ships. Always their numbers were small and their lives were hard. The gold miners came, the ranchers, the farmers, the fishermen, the loggers. The restless people came here, the discontented, the curious and men who were fleeing the cold, the drought, their families, the sheriff and conscription. Almost everything, they found, had to be done to the beat of a different drum here. Usually it was harder to do.

To build roads and railways was as slow as it was also necessary. To this day all transportation, by land or sea, is more expensive than in most parts of earth and in some areas it remains practically impossible. There will probably never be a north-south highway along the western coast. To chisel out ledges along rocky sides of all the fiords scooped out by the glaciers would leave us too exhausted to do anything more. A two-dimensional map conveys little of the reality of the British Columbia situation. Two communities separated by a horizontal distance of fifty miles may be effectively separated by hundreds, for our surface routes must creep around through valleys and over the lowest ridges we may find. Time is frequently substituted for miles in giving estimates of distance and if asked to give directions to a stranger the British Columbian will seldom give them in terms of compass directions—he speaks of roads and trails which bear right or left. The north or south of it means little among the mountains.

Hewing out our foothold in this land took immense effort, a considerable risk and more than the usual quota of optimism. It could never have been done by committees. To this day the practical accomplishments of people outside the metropolitan areas can more often be attributed to energetic doers rather than to thinkers. As the old Scottish song says, mountains divide us and a waste of seas. Here is not one land, but many. There are as many as we may arbitrarily choose to see. My own choice would be a list of nine regions: the Queen Charlotte Islands, Vancouver Island, the mainland coast, the dry belt, the Kootenays, the Peace River country, the northern forest, the northwest corner, and the high country.

The Queen Charlotte Islands, aloof in the misty and windblown sea, have retained an air of detachment not only from the rest of British Columbia but from the world. Wind, fog and rain are its nourishment. There is food in the sea and forest at the beaches. There is one mine. There is a coincidental resemblance to another aloof portion of the world, New Zealand. As with New

Zealand, the Charlottes have a large north island, with broad flat plains, covered here not with sheep and farms but with deer and trees. In both regions is a south island, lonelier, more precipitous. In the Charlottes the settlements of men, now as before, are scattered along a few beach fronts or in small inlets. The interior remains trackless. Indians and the whites who followed them have found their livelihood near the shorelines. They had no reason to hack through the jungle of the rain forest to the islands' centers and the occasional explorer or sportsman who does so is so rare a visitor that his trail is quickly eaten up behind him, overnight it seems, by salal, devil's club and all the other undergrowth which eagerly crowds that damp ground.

Vancouver Island's western beaches and fiords are also largely empty of men. There is a national park on the peninsula shared by the fishing communities of Ucluelet and Tofino and a few other lonely settlements tucked into the long arms of the sea where men mine, make pulp, log or have fishing stations. At Friendly Cove in Nootka Sound, where Macquinna's people first met the whites, there were in the summer of 1976 only three adult whites, operating the federal government lighthouse, and two Indian families in the long line of reserve houses which turn blank windows to the empty cove.

In the southern island and on the southwestern face a line of cities and towns, beginning with Victoria, are knotted along the highway. There are a few farms, mostly given over to pasturing dairy cattle and timberlands which have given up wealth enough to buy kingdoms.

A paved road reached northern Vancouver Island for the first time in 1977 and this, the preserve of loggers, fishermen and a few miners, will now, as we say, open up. Those who went to such fastnesses the hard way, in Union Steamships, by white-knuckle flights in small planes and by picking their way over boulder-strewn logging roads in jeeps and cars, can not with decency regret that tourists of later years shall come like shoals of herring, the sunlight glinting on the sides of their cars and camper trucks. Decency or none, there is some regret for I subscribe to a belief which I first heard voiced by Bob Erlam, publisher of the Whitehorse **Star**, who has seen highways unlock his Yukon country to the flippant and the idly curious of travellers: "My theory is that tourists use up scenery with their eyes. You have to get there before they have looked it over so much they've worn it out."

The mainland coast is a third region. In the Lower Mainland section at the southern end it is so thickly populated that smog obscures much of the land and the density of houses and industrial plants becomes itself landscape and a cause for much trumpeting. Vancouver City proper is shrinking in population, a continent-wide phenomenon, the result of which we cannot perceive but which we may read as one of the most profound social changes of our times. However, residents of the high rise apartments in the city's West End peninsula prefer to believe that their district has a population denser than Hong Kong's and although no statistics support such a notion it is a harmless fancy and there is no reason that it not be indulged.

The first of the fiords begins at the southern edge of the city—Indian Arm. Near here, at Port Moody, the city was originally to have been founded but Canadian Pacific Railway was frightened away by one of the first of our many speculative real estate booms.

The fiords march, one long knobby limb after another, up the stone trunk of the coastline. Here and there the plume of steam from a pulp mill clouds one of the fiords while enabling the people in the comfortable homes of shiny townsites to consider two cars and a pleasure boat to be among the ordinary necessities of life. Northing, lonelier, the forests less patched with logging scars, the land is left to creatures of the woods and sea and at Prince Rupert, the departure point of Alaska Panhandle ferries and the Bering Sea halibut fleets, the rains have washed away almost all the colors to an even gray.

In the great interior dry belt there are no grays except those of old log cabins and long Russel fence lines but there is a monochromatic quality to the landscape that is common wherever the sun beats down on the intermontane dry belt from Mexico to British Columbia.

Here in the first of the several rain shadows, where precipitation is so light that some regions are almost classifiable as desert, grass is seldom green for more than a week or so before toasting to a pale brown. The trees, mostly pine, are scattered lightly on the higher slopes and the dusty earth is pale brown, yellow or occasionally the white of alkali. The lakes and the skies are blue, the rivers brown, blue or, if they be fed rock flour from a source in the glaciers, an emerald green and in autumn the ubiquitous poplar flares to brilliant yellow. But the sun bleaches as it warms this country, which is spectacular in size and shape though never dressed in the blazing colors of eastern Canada's hardwood forests.

The dry belt is the ranch country of the Cariboo, the Chilcotin, the Kamloops and Merritt country. The southernmost extension, the Okanagan and Similkameen valleys, have been irrigated by water and money.

Thus this region, where the Hudson's Bay brigades from the Oregon Territory first wintered their horses, where the dispossessed Mexicans from California came to found the first ranches, is now a place of towns, peach groves, vineyards and carpet factories. In climate, scenery and the pleasant atmosphere that goes with towns which have not yet grown too large, the Okanagan must rank as one of the finest urban living areas of the country and some of us are sorry we didn't buy that valley the first time we saw it. It is too late now, because the price has gone up.

The Kootenays, East and West, are bands of blue mountains sliced north to south by rivers and lakes. They are pocketed with gold, silver, lead, zinc, iron and other metals. In their eastern boundary, the Rockies, are coal fields. None of this wealth came out of the ground easily, but had to be ripped out with machines and explosives. Considering that it was wealth enough to nourish towns living and dead there are surprisingly few scars on the face of that immense land. That there are few scars is not so much a tribute to the care and patience of miners as to the immensity of the land. The old silver mines abandoned on hillfaces through the Lardeau and Kootenay Lake country do not match the devastation left by this generation when it built the hydroelectric dam at Duncan Lake and left the skeletons of a mill on trees in the reservoir.

The forest lands of the central interior are commonly called The North. This is only in part due to the fact that British Columbians who cluster along the 49th parallel are like other Canadians in that anywhere they don't go often is called The North. The center of British Columbia has the feel of north. The carpet of moderate sized trees is spread seamless across rolling hills and shallow valleys, green but brittle with spiky tips which are the mark of trees in regions of heavy snowfalls. Here the winds from the Polar Lands bear down for much of the winter, thrusting aside the gray cloud cover of the Pacific air mass, spilling, occasionally, down the coastal inlets and enveloping the coastal wetlands first in untimely chill and then snowfalls a yard deep. The interior forests, spotted here and there by small towns and the one city of Prince George, are lonely for the most part. They are, once one steps a few hundred yards into the trees, featureless. The sense of direction fades and, if one panics, can be obliterated. Like all coniferous forests they are an almost foodless waste for most wild creatures. Squirrels, whiskey jacks, spruce grouse, porcupine, and a few rabbits never leave these trees. The larger species, like man himself, look for the savannas where leafy things grow.

Wind, trees and sky; and on a horizon when it be seen, stands the lazy mound of yet another ridge of trees. Even more than the rock faces of the Matterhorn-type peaks in the coast range, the central interior forest, like the Barrenlands of the Arctic, arouse admiration, perhaps some love, but always awe in the face of vastness.

The Peace River country, on the other hand, seems part of the Canadian Prairies. British Columbians who have seen a few score miles of waving wheat in the Dawson Creek and Fort St. John districts speak of it as a breadbasket. However, although most things British Columbians say are true they are not said under oath in a witness stand and a degree of caution never hurt any listener.

The Peace produced handfuls of wheat which win prizes in national and international competitions, grown on selected plots by experts. The extent of these wheatlands is scant and at fifty-six degrees north latitude we may wonder if they would survive a moderate fluctuation in annual mean temperatures. Agriculturists say the entire prairie wheat basin to the south is dependent upon an uncertain stability of temperatures and rainfall which have persisted since the drought of the 1930s and the continuation of this climatic regime is not assured. In the Peace, it must be counted less assured. The wealth of the Peace are its natural gas fields, the Alaska Highway which leaves here for the developing Yukon and Alaska regions, the other highway which is soon to cross northeastward into the Mackenzie River valley and, perhaps, the new hydroelectric dams to be built on the Peace River itself.

Men have done little with, or to, the northwest corner of the province. There is one gravel road which reaches north from Hazelton and Terrace to the vicinity of Stewart. It then angles northeastward for 365 lonely miles and connects with the Alaska Highway at Watson Lake in the Yukon. At the extreme northwest corner another road dips south from the Alaska Highway and ends at the old gold rush town of Atlin. Yet another spur road winds through the dessicated canyon of the Stikine River to Telegraph Creek. There is also the provincial railroad which started toward the old fur trading post of Dease Lake until construction stopped in clouds of debt and litigation. These are man's only permanent tracks over one fifth of the area of British Columbia.

Near Stewart, at the Alaska border, is the only spot on all the highway system of British Columbia where a glacier comes close enough to touch and on the almost limitlessly beautiful Iskut Plateau is one of the few areas where a public highway rises above the timberline of our mountains.

The northwest corner is a testing ground for us. Men will go there and we shall develop it, because that is our nature. But so far we have not done so. The opportunity exists, then, for us to avoid the clutter and the mess that have marked so much of our passage in the rest of the land.

Should we fail there, one refuge remains to us in the natural state and this one might last forever. It is the ninth division of the land, all the peaks and the mountain meadows which lie above the upper limits of tree growth. The occasional alpinist, hunter and skier ventures into this Arctic world. Most of us never go there. Unlike the Alps, the Himalayas, the Andes and most other mountainous lands of the earth, men have not yet settled the mountain tops of British Columbia. We live among the mountains, not on them. Perhaps we shall never live there and perhaps we never should but even those who do not go to those regions derive comfort in knowing that they are there.

Much of the joy we take from our land comes from this confidence that the wilderness is nearby and that it is, in some way, our possession. Gold in the bank for us, treasure in Heaven.

For it is wrong to suggest that the life of the British Columbian is a constant struggle with savage, elemental forces. In many ways our lives here are quite the opposite. All settled portions of the coast and offshore islands have climates which are frankly bland. In most areas the winds do not blow fierce nor long and the mists and the rains usually fall gently upon us. Our skies weep, they do not pour. On the coastal mountains, one gray day succeeds the next and rains and fogs are conditions of our lives, not events.

That same condition applies, if in lesser degree, in other parts of the province. The shelf of gray cloud from the Pacific edges far inland and during winters in the Interior, although Arctic air may chill the land to forty below and lower, it can be expected to be succeeded in short time by warm winds from the west.

Neither are our senses assaulted by the impact of scenery ever awesome. Our land is hidden from us much of the time by cloud. Being hemmed in by our mountains, we get the sense of vast spaces only occasionally when we travel high enough to be on the high plateaus or among the higher peaks of the ranges. There is much truth in the prairie farmer's statement that the mountains are nice, but they sure obscure the view. In the valleys, among the forests, our views are much shortened.

This is a land in glorious tumult. Most of us have encountered it only recently and briefly and we have left a few marks on it. We won't shape it much, but it will shape our children and our children's children for as many generations as we last.

Paul St. Pierre.

SPRING

GLACIER LILY   Tom W. Hall

REEDS, NATION LAKES   E. Lavinger

SOURCE OF ST. MARY'S RIVER, PURCELL RANGE

Patrick Morrow

SPRING RAIN, MANNING PARK

R. Herger

FISHING, BELLA COOLA
British Columbia Government

RHODODENDRONS, MANNING PARK

Tom W. Hall

QUEEN ELIZABETH PARK, VANCOUVER   H. Martell

DOUBLE-CRESTED CORMORANTS, GULF ISLANDS

F. Allen

NICOLA LAKE
Clifford A. Fenner

TOD MOUNTAIN, KAMLOOPS

M.O. Kullander

COUGAR, DARCY ISLAND

David Hancock

APE LAKE, CHILCOTIN

Ron Young

SUNSET FROM LIONS GATE BRIDGE   Tony Markle

KANAKA CREEK, MAPLE RIDGE   R. Herger

THREE GUARDSMEN PASS, HAINES HIGHWAY

Duncan Myers

EASTER LILLIES AND SHOOTING STARS
Clifford A. Fenner

KELP, SALT SPRING ISLAND

Nicholas Newbeck

LUPINES IN FOREST BURN, KAMLOOPS
Donovan Clemson

LOG BOOMS, QUEEN CHARLOTTE ISLANDS   Brian Biddlecombe

GROUND SQUIRREL   Mildred McPhee

46

WILLOW PTARMIGAN
GETTING SPRING PLUMAGE   F. Allen

OKANAGAN ORCHARDS   Tom W. Hall

MT. EDZIZA

British Columbia Government

49

BUTTERCUP MEADOW, NANAIMO

Ron Young

SHEPHERD, NORTH OF KAMLOOPS   Donovan Clemson

BLACK BEAR CUB   F. Allen

NETTING SALMON, QUEEN CHARLOTTE ISLANDS

Brian Biddlecombe

MT. ASSINIBOINE

Lance W. Camp

SUMMER

BLACKTAIL DEER FAWN   Charles Whittaker

LAKE OF HANGING GLACIER, PURCELL MTS.
British Columbia Forest Service

PURCELL MOUNTAINS

British Columbia Forest Service

FARWELL CANYON DUNES, CHILCOTIN

Ron Young

David Hancock

TOTEMS, KISPIOX

Marty Loken

GARIBALDI LAKE

H. Martell

RAIN FOREST

British Columbia Forest Service

NEAR HATZIC

Edward M. Gifford

MT. EDZIZA

British Columbia Government

BEAR CREEK FALLS, WELLS GRAY PARK
Donovan Clemson

THUNDERBIRD REGATTA, VICTORIA

James McVie

ELLA COOLA TOTEM POLE
Susan Im Baumgarten

CHINESE FARMERS, FRASER VALLEY

S. Rendall

LEACH LAKE, KOOTENAYS

Madge Gobbett

TUMBLING GLACIER, MT. ROBSON

Lance W. Camp

FRASER CANYON

British Columbia Government

NASS RIVER LAVA BED

Donovan Clemson

CRACROFT

British Columbia Forest Service

SUNSET ON LIGHTNING LAKE, MANNING PARK   R. Herger

LAKE OESA, YOHO PARK   R. Herger

SEASHORE LIFE, QUEEN CHARLOTTE ISLANDS   F. Allen

FARWELL CANYON, CHILCOTIN   Ron Young

NICOLA VALLEY   Donovan Clemson

GULF ISLAND SUNSET
Ed Davis
74 75

HELMCKEN FALLS

Tom W. Hall

"BORDER GUARDIAN", MT. ASSINIBOINE

John J. Anonby

HARVEST AT NEW PAVILION   Leslie Kopas

MOUNTAIN RUNOFF, HAINES CUTOFF　　　　　　　　　F. Allen

ENGLISH BAY　　　　　　　　　Lita Hook

BUGABOOS   Hal Bavin

CAPE SCOTT BEACH
British Columbia Forest Service
82 83

FERNS   F. Allen

MOUNTAIN GOAT   F. Allen

BARK PATTERN   F. Allen

ARBUTUS BARK   Nicholas Newbeck

FOREST FIRE, KAMLOOPS
British Columbia Forest Service

PEACE RIVER VALLEY

Clifford A. Fenner

TULIP CREEK, NEAR CASTLEGAR

Larry Price

CLAM DIGGERS, PATRICIA BAY

David Low

SEA URCHINS   F. Allen

VARIED THRUSH   Bruce A. Macdonald

VANCOUVER   Bruce A. Macdonald

LONG BEACH   Clifford A. Fenner

PACIFIC TREE TOAD   Bruce A. Macdonald

OMINECA VALLEY

British Columbia Government

ROBSON RIVER   Lance W. Camp

PURCELL MOUNTAINS

British Columbia Forest Service

BELLA COOLA VALLEY   Susan Im Baumgarten

CARNEY CREEK

British Columbia Forest Service

PEACE RIVER
Clifford A. Fenner
98 99

100

SPOTTED LAKE, NEAR OSOYOOS

Donovan Clemson

KEREMEOS COLUMNS   Leslie Kopas

THORSEN CREEK PETROGLYPH   Leslie Kopas

FALL

FALL LEAVES   E. Lavinger

BEAR PASS
Clifford A. Fenner

ROCKIES NEAR BRISCO

Patrick Morrow

PUMPKINS   Al Harvey

MISTY TREES, BURNABY   M.D. Hoffman

WASP NEST, MT. ROBSON PARK   Mrs. W. Carson

SURREY FLOOD
Merle Somerville

AUTUMN COLOR   Al Harvey

NICOLA RIVER

Clifford A. Fenner

CHASE   Donovan Clemson

KNUTSFORD
Clifford A. Fenner

112 113

114

HOWE SOUND NEAR SQUAMISH

Ron Young

BRIDGE LAKE

H.D. von Tiesenhausen

VICTORIA
Mike H. Symonds

116

GOLDEN EARS   R. Herger

118

CLINGING HEARTS, BURNABY   M.D. Hoffman

BROHM RIDGE, SQUAMISH

British Columbia Forest Service

SAVONA
Donovan Clemson

Al Harvey

GOLDSTREAM PARK, SPAWNED SALMON
F.W. Wooding

F.L. McLaughlin
SHAGGY MANE MUSHROOM, QUESNEL

WEST SAANICH FRUIT STAND   Al Harvey

WOODS POND, SOOKE

Mrs. W. Carson

MAPLE RIDGE

R. Herger

BEAR GLACIER   Patrick Morrow

HEFFLEY LAKE   Nicholas Newbeck

ALERT BAY   Leslie Kopas

AUTUMN COLOR, BURNABY   M.D. Hoffman

NIMPO LAKE

Clifford A. Fenner

LONG BEACH

Hal Bavin

SELKIRKS EAST OF REVELSTOKE   Donovan Clemson

MAGNA BAY, SHUSWAP LAKE

Donovan Clemson

HOAR FROST, CLINTON   Syd Brown

NICOLA VALLEY
H. Martell

GLACIER SKIING, RADIUM

British Columbia Government

134

BOTANICAL BEACH B. McDougall

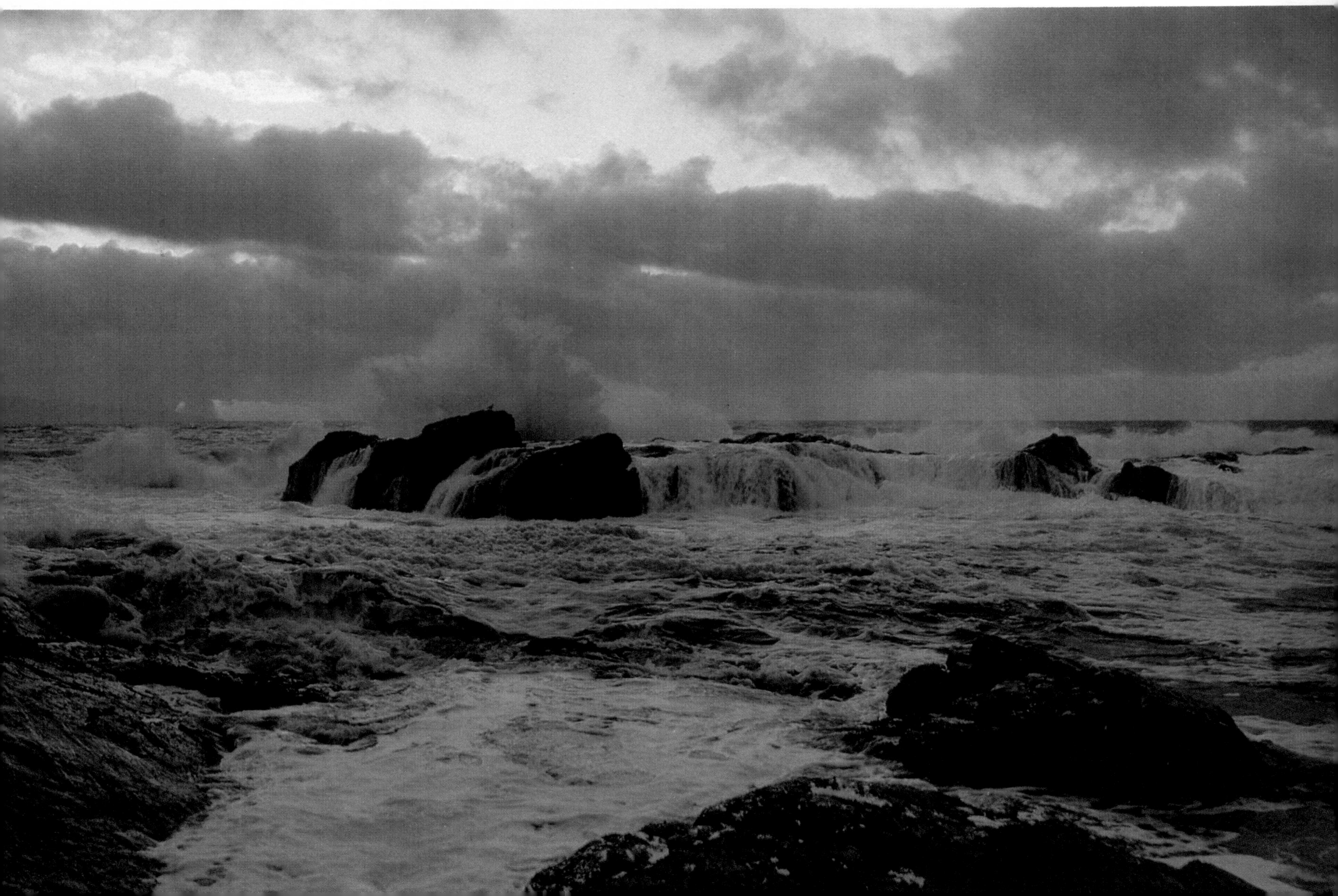

RAVENS, NELSON   Ron Driedger

LAVINA MOUNTAIN

British Columbia Forest Service

THOMPSON RIVER

Clifford A. Fenner

LIGHTHOUSE PARK

I. Moritz

MISSION   H. Martell

CHILCOTIN   F. Allen

 MT. MacDUFF
British Columbia Forest Service

DUNCAN LAKE   British Columbia Forest Service

CRABAPPLES, CARIBOO

Duncan Myers

MT. REVELSTOKE					John G. Woods

ATLIN LAKE   British Columbia Government

148

VALEMOUNT   Mrs. W. Carson

SUNRISE, MT. ASSINIBOINE   Lance W. Camp

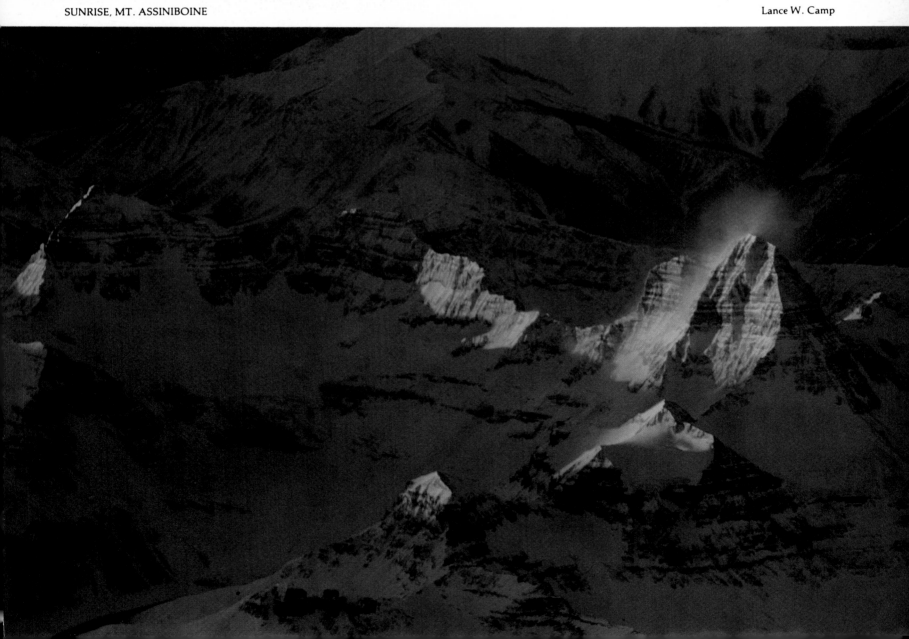

ATLIN

British Columbia Government

UBC, VANCOUVER
H.D. von Tiesenhausen

GARIBALDI PARK   Lance W. Camp

MOUNTAIN GOAT   F. Allen

ELK BROWSING, KOOTENAY RIVER   Patrick Morrow

MT. SEYMOUR   Lance W. Camp

SAWMILL, YELLOWHEAD HIGHWAY   M.E. Wooding

GALIANO GALLERIES
F. Allen
154

155

FROSTY LEAVES, MAPLE RIDGE   R. Herger

VANCOUVER   Edward M. Gifford

KICKING HORSE RIVER

Patrick Morrow

ILLISILLOETTE RIVER, REVELSTOKE   Michael Sturdy

LONESOME LAKE SWANS

Trudy and Jack Turner

108 MILE RANCH

British Columbia Forest Service